MUSEUM HOURS

MUSEUM HOURS

MICHAEL KELLEHER

BLAZEVOX[BOOKS]
Buffalo, New York

Museum Hours
by Michael Kelleher
Copyright © 2017

Published by BlazeVOX [books]

Printed in the United States of America

Interior design and typesetting by Geoffrey Gatza
Cover Art by Lara Odell

First Edition
ISBN: 978-1-60964-243-3
Library of Congress Control Number: 2015959390

BlazeVOX [books]
131 Euclid Ave
Kenmore, NY 14217

Editor@blazevox.org

publisher of weird little books

BlazeVOX [books]

blazevox.org

21 20 19 18 17 16 15 14 13 12 01 02 03 04 05 06 07 08 09 10

BlazeVOX

Acknowledgments

Some of the poems in this book appeared in *The Brooklyn Rail*, *Sentence: A Journal of the Prose Poem*, and *Kadar Koli*. Thanks respectively to Anselm Berrigan, Richard Deming, David Hadbawnik for choosing to publish them.

TABLE OF CONTENTS

MUSEUM HOURS

EKPHRASIS

ARS MEMORIA

Picture if you will a room. With bright white walls.

Infinitely tall. Sunlight from a source above pours in.

Whiteness swells until it nearly burns the eyes.

If not quite. If not for a series of dark squares.

Every several feet on each of the walls. Which.

At first glance one could be forgiven for thinking.

Were afterimages. *After* what one is left to puzzle out.

As these dark squares come into focus. Picture.

If you will a man or woman. Or let's just say yourself.

Whoever you are. Standing in front of a square.

A tiny thing. Your upright organism. Your body.

About as significant now as a spear of grass in a field.

Swaying. This should give you a sense of the magnitude.

Of the room that you find yourself standing in. A room.

Connected to other rooms. Of equal or greater size.

By a network of passages. That in concert form.

A whole. Of which they're each a part. I am speaking.
Of course. Of the museum. A place to see. Not just to see.
But to be. And be in. To inhabit and wander through.
Endlessly. Endlessly.

NATURE MORT

1. *I and Thou* by Martin Buber and beneath it

2. *The Gate* by Natsume Soseki and beneath that

3. *And Then,* also by Soseki, which ends with the color red burning through the mind of the protagonist, a man on a tram who sees a red mailbox, four red umbrellas spinning, a vendor selling bright red balloons, a red automobile passing, a tobacconist's red curtain, a red banner announcing a sale, a red telephone pole, and, finally, the whole world turns red and starts to spin, and the man decides to go on riding until his head has burned completely away and to the left, atop another pile

4. *Self-Portrait in a Convex Mirror* by John Ashbery, which I reread to counter a book by Frank Bidart called

5. *Metaphysical Dog* that rests on top of

6. John Berger's *Ways of Seeing,* which contains a long discussion of a painting by Hans Holbein the Younger called *The Ambassadors,* that hangs in the National Gallery of London, I saw it once, the

difference between what I had seen on the page in black and white, and the object itself, its magnificent detail, the richness of its colors, the bizarre anamorphic skull at the bottom of the canvas, which can hardly be deciphered on the page, you sort of have to be there to see it, and I am glad that I was and under Berger

7. *The Collected Poems of William Carlos Williams, Volume II* and then, atop a third stack, to the left of the first

8. *Believing is Seeing,* essays by Errol Morris that I read when they appeared on a blog at the Times and which was given to me as a gift that I have to admit I have not gone back to read and under it

9. *Selected Poems* of Auden, from which I read his "Museé de Beaux Arts" alongside Williams' "Landscape with the Fall of Icarus" after having watched a film called *Museum Hours* in which Breughel's paintings feature prominently and about which I wrote a poem called, "Icarus (Redux)" plus

10. *Illuminations* by Walter Benjamin

11. *Odas Elementales* by Pablo Neruda

12. *Selected Poems* by Francis Ponge

13. *Collected Poems* by Stephan Mallarmé

14. *Fantasias in Counting* by Sophie Seita, who gave me her book a while back and beside these

15. a pair of notebooks

16. a failed application for a home equity loan

17. three blank sheets of paper in the printer tray

18. the printer

19. two black felt-tip pens leaning in

20. a pewter mug I was given as a gift for bartending at a wedding

21. two CD's by Damian I've been meaning to listen to

22. the shiny metal desk lamp

23. my laptop tucked into

24. a stand into which are plugged

25. the keyboard and

26. the mouse and beneath them all

27. the wooden desktop, which I bought many years ago and which hasn't aged at all despite the fact I've moved seven times since and sat at it every day reading, writing, looking at the internet, and staring out

28. the window at

29. the trees and looking down at the desktop I notice a small set of what could be

30. hieroglyphs but which are actually impressions left in the wood by the tip of one of my pens as it pressed into a thin sheet of paper whatever my thoughts and/or feelings might have been on that occasion but which are now indecipherable even and especially to myself.

LANDSCAPE WITH FIGURES

The great blue curve of the sea, a whip

about to crack, draws the eye to the horizon.

A river of human flotsam, *okeanos,*

encircles the world. Pale bodies cook

prone or supine beneath the sun

or step into water drained of color

to such an extent the mind fails

to register relief, real or imagined,

from this ubiquitous, depth-destroying light.

If you listen close you can almost hear

the cancers being born, cell by cell,

beneath oozing dollops of sunblocker.

The eye, in search of a place to rest

among an infinity of striped umbrellas,

finds no purchase. A thick black line

divides the image in two, or so it seems.

Traces of things: an arm, a leg,

a checkered towel, a life preserver,

repeat themselves on either side.

My stereoscopic eye would make them one,

but the image resists completion,

insists on its doubling. A border. An edge.
Edge among edges. Blue becomes white
becomes yellow becomes green. The coughing
gray cloud of the city rises in the distance.
Beyond it, the mountains. Yes, the sublime.

WEATHER REPORT

Today I thought of the future, and the future was in the machines. I heard the growl of a leopard and started to run. It was all somehow predestined. First, realism, then the reaction to realism.

Nobody knows it's the end of an age. Peaches like sinister rain clouds. The frozen landscape speeding by. What was the first cause?

The days came and went and no one spoke. I ran around the house, calling after the cats. I was in love. And what comes after that? To return was unimaginable. A crystalline cold invades the home. Beyond the window, words.

Same sun, different day. It's all right there: the delicate colors, the lately struck keys of a piano. A bony finger indicates the water. From the liquid element springs a myth. The oceans recede and we know the room is violet. I have heard the rattle of my breathing.

Blue is the color that best expresses the mood. A crude hunger clears the land. The language of America overflows. Do you believe in magic? Will you remember me when I die?

The clouds that come from me and the clouds that cover me comfort me. A pause. A promise of money. The sky on my head. I find it hard to trace these changes.

I mean I haven't a plan. I mean I like remembering.

EKPHRASIS

The mind, freely

responding, strives

to form an image

made of words, from

its apprehension of

their meaning, not

definition alone, but

context, sound,

experience, memory,

sense, how foolish

one is to think

to make a picture

made of words,

magical figments

to dazzle the mind,

and yet the image

persists, lives on

as ghosts of past lives

live on, long past

their usefulness,

fixed in place,

a sacred hologram

or puny three

-dimensional god,

insignificant and

utterly false, who

must be reckoned

with, ultimately,

finally, at last.

THE WHITE HORSE

A White Horse is Not a Horse,

A Painted Deer is not a Deer,

by artist Cheng Shifa,

'currently not on display,'

depicts a woman and two deer

as well as some writing in Chinese.

The title, I suppose. Or not.

I struggle to see detail

inside this tiny digital box.

The image will not expand.

Where is the white horse?

If such a creature exists

it is not visible at this scale.

I'm not so much concerned

with the existence of the horse.

What holds my attention

is the title. I keep asking myself

why the horse is white.

Is there a horse in the painting

so white it can't be seen?

Or does this mean

that whiteness makes the horse

another species altogether?

I am reminded of another title

I once wanted to steal,

from a painting by Joan Miró:

People at Night, Guided by

the Phosphorescent Traces of Snails.

The title is so good

you don't even need a painting.

Just picture a network

of slimy trails shimmering

in the moonlight, and giving chase,

a band of humans, forever

after the secret of their art.

ANOTHER WHITE HORSE

Blue slices of sky

almost unbearable as rain

rips through a seam.

Black clouds swirl

about the center.

Mountains huddle

unaffected in silhouette.

The chickens, the dog,

the white horse, perhaps

called to attention

by thunder, turn their

backs to us, as if

they can see the future.

I feel a sudden chill.

The firewood's cut

and neatly stacked

in piles beside the barn.

PORTRAIT OF THE POET IWAR VON LÜCKEN BY OTTO DIX, 1926

A tall, gaunt, middle-aged man backs into the corner of a garret. A grimy urban sunset purples in the window, through which can be seen an outsize angel on a cathedral spire, the poet's dirty brown suit two sizes too large, his grey transparent eyes alcoholic slits.

What stand out most are the fingers of Iwar von Lücken. Spectral, misshapen, freakishly long, they might have been broken and poorly repaired more than once. Their natural form, whatever it may have been, is unrecognizable. The right hand hangs at his side, palm facing the painter, as if to ask when this will all be over. Not just the sitting. All of it.

It's hard to tell what holds him up, whether he is leaning against a wall in the expressionistic corner, or balancing on the gangly flexion of his knees, or if the left hand grasping the coat on the back of the chair sustains his weight. My eyes are drawn to the seat, a makeshift pedestal for a makeshift vase for a bouquet of actual yellow roses, an ornament or symbol, no doubt, perhaps the soul of the poet, the immortal beauty hidden in his shabby, collapsing frame.

He left behind one slim volume of poems, ignored during his lifetime and after. Only two copies exist, both of them housed in the libraries of Berlin, untranslated. A thought passes that I should travel there, be the one who brings this forgotten poet back to life for English readers, but I don't speak German and I can't afford the ticket to Berlin.

Two other portraits of von Lücken exist. The first is a lithograph of the poet from the waist up, seated, body turned slightly to the right. His wide open eyes register something between shock and wonder. A crooked finger presses lightly against his cheek. It seems everyone noticed those sinewy, angular digits.

The second is a sketch from his volume of poems, *Gedichte*, in which we see him from the neck up, again the fingers, four of them, nuzzle into the folds of his face. His head faces the viewer while his tender sodden eyes, refusing contact, gaze nervously out of the frame, half-amused, half-embarrassed, or maybe just thinking of something else. An empty bottle filled with roses on a chair.

ZERO GRAVITY (A HOAX)

First thing I read this morning

said tomorrow, January 4, 2015,

my mother's 78th birthday,

at 9:57 a.m. Pacific Standard Time,

the planets would align in such a way

that for five minutes gravity,

that fundamental fact, that force

that gives everything weight (gravitas),

would momentarily render all objects

weightless. We'd be able to float,

like in that painting by Chagall

in which the artist celebrates

a birthday with his wife

in their modest apartment.

On a table by the window

sit a cake, a knife, a mug, a plate.

Through the glass one sees the street

obscured in one pane by a reflection

of the interior: a stool, a bed, a tapestry

on the wall. The woman holds

in her hand a bouquet, a gift, I suspect.

She floats. A flight of ecstasy, perhaps.

Likewise the man, whose lack of gravity

makes him supple as an eel

through water as he wraps himself

around her from behind and plants

a weightless kiss upon her lips.

Her eyes open wide with surprise,

or wonder, or possibly concern.

Is the kettle on? Did she feed the cat?

Or maybe they've widened because

she senses gravity's burden will return

to her limbs, she'll feel its pull, its

pulling her back down to earth.

JOYFUL MOUNTAIN LANDSCAPE

If I could measure memory, map it out,

transform the hours between events

into coordinates and lay them on a grid

with lines of longitude and latitude,

a legend to signal the scale of time,

a compass rose to indicate the poles,

I would commence with the form of a tree

rising, joyous and alone, between

two mountain peaks, the sun and moon

would float improbably across the sky

and cast a twilit winter pink upon the hills,

and from this tree would everything unfold,

eternal origami, its leaves would have fallen

and blown away, I would think of this

as evidence of change, a narrative

progressing to its end, and I would lean in

to look more closely, to see this cycle

as one among many now spreading

across the rugged topography, memories

by the millions flooding up through the map,

my mother's eyes, my father's voice, sounds

and smells of everyone I've ever loved,

it would all seem too much, a crashing wave

that overwhelms, and then I would retreat

to a clean Euclidean space, I'd fix my gaze

upon the earth around the tree, the ground

which gives it life, a place to stand, and which

later, much later, will become its place of rest,

and the colors would reveal themselves, and I

would see them and be them, become the light

with which they are imbued, and I could say,

after Klee, that "color and I are one."

HELIOTROPE

1

No clouds, just wind. And bulldozers scraping

the sea. A theme: the space between the words.

The interval. Daubs of water wash out

the sky. The whiteness flattens everything.

Suspended gestures, lost in the blue.

2

Where the object ends, micro-ambient:

a floppy summer hat, tilted just so.

A picture window by a TV set.

A sound, as of tearing, through or into.

And then release: the trees in silhouette.

3

The car makes a turn, ends up in Texas.

It's a big state, but we'll have to share it.

Tarantulas, cowboys, marionettes.

All those Cadillacs buried in the dirt.

Heroes in miniature shine in their spurs.

4

A girl in a glass house listens to

Horace Silver, 1976.

Eclipse, full moon, slippery roads outside.

The music full blast. Oranges, yellows, reds.

The fundamentals. A private lesson.

5

The calm before the room begins to spin.

Each object in proper gravitation:

at rest, unmoved. Attraction has its pulls.

And then the roof gives way to stars,

the moon so close, so cold, I could kiss it.

6

The light illumines particles. Alive,

they dance. The palette must acidify.

Impossible greens in the powder's glow.

Between the thought and the arrival of

its purpose. Call it the author's intent.

7

Sea-green earrings, a tremor of tulips.

A ladder climbing blindly to the sky.

Why we never speak of seismographs, faults,

Shifts in the plates. Wordless, California

exhales, slips silently into the sea.

8

Time presses on, successive visitors

find a hostess unprepared, out of booze,

gussied up for no one. Little histories

of paper, wrappers, checkbooks, and mirrors.

An object lesson: this, this, this, and this.

9

This day is for nothing, for atmosphere.

A day to get away from making lists.

To find a rhythm. A day for snow.

A snow day. Quiet blankets everything.

Nothing is sacred. Reading is futile.

10

Tight-fisted, the war comes rushing back:
those hideous faces beautifully drawn.
Clouds dissolve into cocktails of blather.
To love: the silent ocean, flat and still.
The inner logic of the sea: it's cold.

11

The rising water floods the underground

museum. It all piles up, accumulates:

a renaissance of sorts. I wet my brush.

A cold wind seeps through the cracks in the stone.

Her yellow petals swim against the tide.

12

Towards evening, the rapture of the weld,

of piecing it together: my kingdom

of steel. Palms upward, I dream of a man:

a doctor. He's standing in a garden,

but there isn't a garden to stand in.

13

All the while I'm thinking after a phrase.

Hydrangeas shine beneath the moon: they'd grown

there flowering, nameless, for years until

I named them. From the Greek: *water vessel.*

At last: no embellishments, no parasols.

14

The official owl rises at dawn, hoots,

then flies off. The variegated grasses,

the dog hunting backyard prey, ice blue eyes

alert. The voice of struggle whispers on

the wire: *I was born this day, born this day.*

15

Throw everything out, start again, design

a form, a shape, imagine it in three

dimensions. Then bring the object to life.

Or did I mean bring it back to life?

Was it always there, waiting to be seen?

16

The sun bursts in through five translucent panes.

Its rays, or radii, radiant.

The loneliness spreads itself, virus-like,

throughout the house, returns to me: a dream

of nothingness. A miracle of form.

17

Here the language of description breaks down.

Four syllables, two beats. Then wakefulness.

The passage from sleep to some other state.

Again I'm turning toward the sound, the sun.

An engine grinds. I reach for my idea.

OLTW

These poems were written in response to a documentary photo project by Rachel Sussman called *The Oldest Living Things in The World*. Since 2004, Sussman has traversed the globe, photographing continuously living organisms more than 2,000 years old.

STROMATOLITES

Arms splayed wide as if to grasp

each other's hands, if never quite

to touch, a large extended family

of gingerbread men lies face down

in shallow water, apparently drowned.

The sky is clear and oh so blue,

a gorgeous day in Western Australia,

not atypical either. I remember

wandering the streets of Sydney

(in the east), everything out of whack,

time most of all. My internal clock

read eight p.m. yet the sunlight shone

at noon the following day. Nevertheless

the gingerbread men of western OZ

are very much alive. Two thousand-plus

years old, these layered biochemical

accretionary structures form

in shallow water as biofilms trap,

bind, and cement sedimentary grains

of microorganisms. The name combines

stroma and *lithos,* "mattress" and "stone."

I picture the man who named them

standing, Whitmanic, above this

bay of sleep, wondering to himself

or possibly aloud if the line between

life and death isn't so very clear, if

it even exists, thinking too it might be

time to catch a nap before setting himself

to the tasks he's planned for the afternoon.

LA LLARETA

These densely packed buds

on long, thin stems cling

to each other with such ferocity

that what we see resembles not

so much a flower as *The Blob*,

that mysterious organism

deposited by meteor to earth,

which feeds and grows voraciously

on human flesh, its only weakness

the cold, a fact discovered

by a young Steve McQueen,

who escapes the fate of so many

in Anytown, USA

when he hides from the monster

in a walk-in restaurant cooler,

but the Llareta plant of Chile,

(or the Atacama Desert, to be

exact, a place compared often

to Mars or the moon) despite

its otherworldly appearance,

bears humankind no malice,

its bulbous muscularity,

though it may appear alien

to the outsider, is at home

here in the high mountain sand,

providing fuel to the fires

of rangers and nomads,

it warms them from the chill

nighttime winds that blow

out of who-knows-where,

some even use them as chairs

or platforms to stand upon,

perhaps to get a better view,

perhaps to test their strength,

amazed to learn a million flowers

can over time grow so close

they shed their tender selves

to form a collective bond

that reverses time's passage,

making them stronger, firm

in their resolve to outlast

every living thing in sight.

ANTARCTIC MOSS

As we pick over the bones

of long dead whales, ocean's

dried detritus, dense white clouds

descend upon the mountain

like a judgment, smothering

its peak, its wide brown flanks,

leaving visible only a thin belt

of soft green moss tensed

around its waist. Is it the subtle

daily encroachments of the sea

that frighten them? Fear of

invisibility? Of being swallowed

and blinded by the cloud?

Surely it isn't Leviathan,

whose bleached and broken bones,

having rendered up their colors

as supplication and ornament,

are little more than provender.

It must be something else,

something not in the frame

yet framing it, the threat

of an ending, the possibility

of which has just begun

to be revealed, but hasn't yet

a proper name.

BRISTLECONE PINE

Some poems grow slowly,

one line at a time,

one word at a time,

one silence. Certain climes

or altitudes lack

the readers necessary

for steady growth,

causing poems to conserve

energy by shutting down.

Indeed, some poems grow

at a remarkably slow rate,

one letter per century,

say, and can survive

with few if any readers

for up to 5,000 years.

One cannot surmise

their age by size alone.

Many express themselves

in short lines or tiny fonts

whose efficient use

of space makes growth

nearly imperceptible.

Evidence of longevity

is often buried deep inside,

rendering most scientific

dating methods moot. Yet,

despite the mystery

of their provenance,

despite the fact that by all

outward signs these poems

are but fossilized remains,

it is not unheard of,

in the rarefied zones

these organisms inhabit,

to discover a family of rhymes

not merely surviving

but thriving. One has to marvel

at their ability to adapt

to a habitat in which so few

readers even know they exist,

fewer still even care.

MAP LICHEN

If asked, I'd say no, there is

no relation between

the random patterns produced

by climate-dependent lichen

as they spread across the surface

of a stone in some barren place

like southern Greenland

and the visual renderings

of land masses known as maps,

even less so the boundaries

drawn between nation-states,

and yet these pareidolia,

in which we see or hear or feel

or better yet divine meaning

where there is none, might be

nothing more than involuntary

projections, that is, human beings

may have developed the skill

over time to quickly recognize

a face as friend or foe, and yet

applied to non-human features,

this adaptation seems at best

a leftover contrivance

that hinders rather than expands

our understanding of the world,

in other words, we liken the lichen

to a map because it pleases us

to connect two unfamiliar things

in familiar terms, to draw

an arbitrary yet to our minds

meaningful line between

the adumbrations of change

and the ostensibly self-determined

march of human progress, so that

wherever we look we see ourselves,

most often in a kindly light,

innocent and ever-improving

organisms whose activities

are but benign responses

to our environments, because

it would be too much to bear,

would it not, if the face of Jesus

we see on the surface of Mars,

or the cartographic patterning

of the *rhizocarpon geographicum,*

were nothing more than

evolution's sleight-of-hand,

a trick the eye plays on the mind

or vice-versa.

PANDO (A THOUSAND PLATEAUS)

Thick, black horizontal scars

and prominent black knots

mark the smooth, white skin

of the *populus tremuloides*.

Not a tree but a clone, it spreads,

just as the name of this grove,

the literal translation of which

("I spread") suggests a unitary mind

diffusing rhizomatically ("a rhizome

has no beginning or end"). Pushing

itself sideways and down, it holds

its place without ever standing still,

sends scouts outward in the form

of green shoots that rise quickly.

The fibers shred and expand, gaining

strength in proportion to the damage

("the fabric of the rhizome is

the conjunction, and....and....and....").

Having multiplied into an army of giants,

it sends feelers in all directions,

antennae taking measure of the light,

the vibrations of the breeze.

Sound waves crossing the universe

cause the leaves to quake, quietly

at first, then louder, in unison,

a million chattering castanets

turn yellow from green

before falling to the ground,

one, two, three thousand at once,

then nothing, the passage of time,

eighty-thousand-maybe-a-million years

 ("variation, expansion, conquest,

capture, offshoots.").

PLOWBREAKER

Rued by farmers,

out of reach by fire,

they procure water

from the depths. Hard

yellowish cream prickles

scatter along the veins

of the leaf. Hundreds

possibly thousands

of years old, they surface

by way of a colony

of what appear to be

independent growths.

Autumn leaves masked

by chlorophyll glut

latently hold back

their stealthy hues.

Leaf scars fashioned

by the plant seal stem

wounds (housekeeping).

The sturdy wood

suffrutex stores resources

underground. (At one time
asthmatics smoked
the dried stems in hope
of relief.) They wait for a fast
robust regeneration until winter
bursts into spring
the plowbreaker flowers
in scarlet terminal racemes
the calyx a five-lobed tube
from which petals emerge.
Neither farmers nor fire
nor drought can kill
these subterranean forests.
Still, the rumor of a road
spreading over the burnt red
clay will not be quelled.

NEPTUNE GRASS

Low-cost acoustic sensing

for freshwater bodies.

A trance remix. What is called

"the ear beneath the sea,"

discovered by an Englishman

who told us why the sky is blue.

Across the surface glides

the surfer with such ease

one wonders does he know

what lives beneath his feet.

Should he care? Sunlight pushes

through the crashing crests.

The onlookers fear their lives

are ruled by supernatural forces:

gods of the sky, gods of the earth,

gods of the sea (the underworld),

and who can blame them?

It's all so deep. The lifeguard

argues we should look inside

ourselves to find the answers,

so we do, and discover there

an ocean, mysterious and vast,

a cliché that fascinates us anyway.

Our subject finally comes

into view: it is time or rather

amplitude. On the ocean floor

an endless field of swaying grass,

the fronds of which absorb

the light as luminescent fish

flit through shadows. Sounds

scatter (or is it my attention?).

The sea, the sea again is racing,

racing towards the shore.

OLD TJIKKO

It appears from this angle

and distance little more

than a ragged stick, rising

weakly, staggering over

a moonscape of stone,

at a glance no different

from the broken pines

beside our house

which lost their tops

in superstorms and such.

The caption reads:

Spruce Gran Picea #0909-11A07

(9,550 years old; Sweden).

Thus, this teetering trunk

(a stunted shrub

for most of its life, they say

it came to resemble a tree

only with the advent

of Global Warming)

had stood its ground, silent

and mostly ignored

as empire after empire

burst into flames, until,

that is, a geologist,

serendipitously named Leif,

used carbon dating

to discover its age

before he christened it

with the appellation

of his late, beloved dog.

WELWITSCHIA MIRABILIS

Having passed the day,

the month, the year,

the decade, the century,

the millennium living

in the harshest conditions,

one can imagine this

miraculous plant, a genus

unto itself, its many heads

buried in as many breasts,

long green fronds

flattened to the sand,

has finally succumbed

to time. Its demeanor

suggests nothing less

than capitulation. As if

to say, Enough! And yet

from another perspective...

Imagine if you will

a ballerina who, having

finished her dance

collapses breathlessly

into a bow, legs crossed,

stifling triumphant tears

into her chest, grateful

but contained, which seems

closer in spirit to this

monotypic gymnosperm,

whose heads will eventually

rise doggedly up against

the punishing sun, a single word,

a botanical manifesto, on its lips.

MUSEUM HOURS

January 2104

Dear Yuko Otomo,

I would like to write a book like your *Study* someday. I picture myself going daily to a museum and selecting a different picture to observe. I take notes, then return home to write poems. I do this every day until I have enough to fill a book. In the process I learn a lot about art.

Which is more or less what I've done while reading *Study*, except that in this case I substituted your book for a real museum. I read a few pages each day, Googled images of the art, took notes in the margins. I followed a fairly strict routine through the first section of the book, reading a cycle of poems in the morning and looking at images by the artists later in the day. At night, I reread the poems, using only my memory of the images as a guide.

The routine varied somewhat as I moved through the book. Even though many of the artists were familiar to me, I couldn't recall specific works. Others were totally unfamiliar. I decided to look first and read second or in some cases to switch back and forth between looking and reading. My eyes roamed from the image on my screen to the book on my desk and back.

One night I watched a movie about Ray Johnson after reading your poem about him. It was called, *How to Draw a Bunny*.

February 2014

It's been a month since I started this letter, but I haven't finished it because I keep returning to *Study*, as if to a memory palace, to immerse myself in your experience of art.

The low, mid-winter sun blasts through a large, south-facing window. I have to hold up my left hand to shield my eyes while I read your Robert Frank poems.

Trolley–New Orleans makes me think of the Tennessee Williams' play *A Streetcar Named Desire*. In an archive at the Beinecke Library, where I work, I once found an actual ticket to the actual streetcar named *Desire* from around the time the play was written. It's a much more interesting artifact than the autographed Playbill it fell out of.

I picture the fluttering curtains in *View from Hotel Window –
Butte Montana* to be actually fluttering. In the photo I see
that they are still.

***

My first memory of poetry (and painting) has to do with
Seurat. Growing up I spent Saturday mornings in front of
the television watching cartoons. Educational PSAs called
Snippets sometimes aired between *Bugs Bunny* and *Scooby-
Doo*. One of them featured Seurat's *A Sunday Afternoon on
the Island of La Grande Jatte*.

They filmed the painting from a distance so that you could
see the whole picture before they zoomed in to reveal that
it had been painted using thousands of individual dots.
They used the word Pointillism, and made a point of
repeating it. The *Snippet* ended with a short mnemonic
poem intoned by a woman with a British accent:

*Seurat
Knew a lot
About dots*

***

You mention the date of a Bruce Nauman Exhibition you attended: 4.4.1995. On that date, I was in Quito, Ecuador doing a year of volunteer teaching. A number of significant events occurred in America while I was there that felt more remote to me than they did to my friends back in the states. The Republican takeover of congress. The OJ Simpson trial. The Oklahoma City bombing.

On the table in the midst of
a violent incident
flowers in a vase
remain flowers

I watch a video clip of Nauman's *A Violent Incident.* I hear the man say, "You fucking cunt! Don't you ever--" She throws water in his face. She knees him in the balls. The flowers on the table are yellow. Possibly they are tulips or unopened roses. It's hard to tell because the grainy image in the video is of a television on which the video of *A Violent Incident* is playing.

***

Max Beckmann's blacks
like cracks

in the sky you
fall into.

***

I try to figure out which *Untitled* painting by Cy Twombly
you are writing about, then realize it doesn't matter.

A massive snowstorm falls outside my window.

***

The verisimilitude of the eyes in Lippo Lippi's paintings
establishes contact across the centuries. I feel like they can
see me nearly as clearly as I see them. I wonder if it is
Lippi himself staring back at me.

***

I am aware of myself sitting at my desk reading. The
room's only light enters through a sliding glass door.
Despite the gray winter sky, it feels crisp and bright
because the ground is covered in snow. I feel compelled to

get closer to it. I stand up, holding *Study* in my hand, and walk towards the light. I lean against the glass as I read the rest of the poem I had been reading, *Tracing Time With 2BS and 3BS*.

August 2014

Recently, I saw a movie called *Museum Hours*, by Jem Cohen. It reminded me of everything I loved about your book. The film centers on a brief friendship that develops between two solitary people, one a middle-aged Canadian woman, the other a (late) middle-aged Austrian man.

We don't know much about the woman, except that her cousin, who she appears to have met only once, lies in a coma in a Vienna hospital. The woman's phone number was the only one the doctors found in her cousin's possession, so they called her. We see her from behind, standing at a window while talking with someone on the phone. A sibling perhaps. She tells the person on the phone that she must go to Vienna and asks to borrow money. We don't know what the woman does for a living or who this relative is or why she bothers to travel to

Vienna to observe the passing of someone she's hardly known.

However, we do learn a bit about the man, mostly through his first-person narration. He works as a security guard at the Kunsthistorisches Museum. He tells us that as a young man he worked security in the music industry and had a lot of fun. We also learn that he is not a passive observer. He pays close attention to both the art he protects and the people who come to look at it. His observations sound like journal entries read aloud.

The woman, who knows no one in Vienna, comes often to the museum, presumably because she has no money and the museum doesn't charge admission. The guard observes her fumbling with a map of the city. He approaches and asks if he can help. She doesn't know how to get to the hospital where her cousin is dying. He gives her directions and offers to show her around town, even to translate over the phone with the doctor. In one of many asides he tells us that he makes this latter offer in order to verify that she isn't running a scam.

The friendship that grows between them forms the emotional core of the film. We accompany them as they visit the hidden corners of Vienna. We listen in on their conversations as they sit in a cafe. We watch as they dance in a bar. Sometimes they sit together at the bedside of her cousin. The woman likes to sing to her cousin and has a lovely voice. I read that the actress who plays the woman is, in real life, a singer.

If their relationship forms the emotional center of the film, the Kunsthistorisches Museum forms the aesthetic and intellectual one. We learn from the guard that the museum houses one of the most impressive collections of Bruegel in the world as well as some choice Rembrandts and Arcimboldos. The director uses works of art to deepen our understanding of the story and its characters. In several scenes the camera cuts back and forth between paintings and carefully composed shots that echo what we see in the paintings without attempting to recreate them.

The guard tells us about the different ways the patrons respond to naked human bodies depicted in art, how the context of the gallery allows them to enjoy erotic feelings without shame. He wryly comments that a lot of the art in the museum is actually pornographic. As he says this, the camera moves from one nude to another, then shifts its view to the various patrons observing these nudes. They are men and women, young and old, skinny and fat.

The camera lingers for enough time on each face that when it returns to the first, we recognize the slender young woman with elongated Renaissance features and dark, straight hair. The camera moves slowly down her naked body, then cuts away. One by one the same patrons we've seen observing these nudes, men and women, old and young, skinny and fat, appear without their clothes. The camera asks us to look at their bodies as they look at the bodies in the paintings. It asks us to feel erotic without shame.

In another scene a docent gives a tour of the Breughel room to a small group of English-speaking tourists. It lasts almost ten minutes and raises many questions, for instance about the universality and timelessness of art, the tension between the laymen's presumed understanding of representational art and his feelings of helplessness, bewilderment, even rage in the face of modern and contemporary art, and also about the ways in which money and class permeate the creation and appreciation of art through the ages.

(In another clever aside, the guard shares with us his memory of a college student who worked with him for a summer, droning on about 'late capitalism.' The guard is impressed with his knowledge, but wonders also if his class consciousness isn't keeping him from understanding some larger truths about art.)

The film spends so much time inside the museum that after a while I could feel the height of the ceilings and I could hear the sound of shoes stepping over the floors and I could see the colors on the walls and the details around the doors and I could imagine standing in the Bruegel room for hours. It began to feel like a place I had visited many times, or a memory of that place.

There is not much else to say about the two main characters. The cousin dies and the friendship comes to its natural end because the woman must return home.

***

November 2014

(Ars Memoria)

I daydream about making a miniature theater for my
daughter. I use an empty shoebox that is at this moment
sitting on the floor of the garage as a kind of proscenium.
I tear up an old t-shirt to make curtains. I paint a set on
the inside and use my daughter's Lego figures for actors. I
write a play based on her current favorite book. It's called
Emily's Balloon. She loves balloons and it so happens her
name is Emily. We named her after the poet. The story
goes like this:

A little girl's mother buys her a yellow balloon from a
street vendor. She lets go. The balloon flies away. She's
sad. Her mother buys Emily another balloon and ties it to
her finger. They walk home. She lets it go again inside the
house and it rises to the ceiling. Her mother ties a small
spoon to the end of the string so that the balloon floats
just off the ground without flying away. Emily carries the
balloon out to the garden. She crowns herself with a
garland of flowers. A gust of wind carries the balloon up
to a tree, well out of reach. Emily cries. She tells her

mother all the things she would have done with the balloon if she still had it. They would have eaten dinner together, brushed their teeth together, gone to bed together. Her mother promises to get it down tomorrow. Emily can't sleep. She looks out her window and sees the yellow balloon still stuck in the limb of the tree. It looks like the moon.

The End.

January 2015

I have been writing this letter for over a year. It keeps getting longer, so that it feels like I might never complete it. Hard to imagine ever sending it to you. Perhaps I will someday. It seems so archaic, this idea of writing and sending a letter, what with the easy communication enabled in digital space. But then, who would ever take a year to write an email or a tweet or a Facebook post? A letter is the only form that allows for slow composition (decomposition?).

The last thing I wanted to tell you was that I did try to do what I imagined at the beginning of this missive. It was in summer. Several days a week, during my lunch break, I went to the art gallery and strolled around looking for subjects for my poems. The painting I came back to again and again was *Le Café de Nuit*, by Vincent Van Gogh. You are probably familiar with it. I'll try to describe it anyway.

As the title suggests, the setting is a cafe at night. The dominant colors are yellow, red, and green, all of them layered on thickly, violently, as if Van Gogh wanted to make you feel nauseous looking at them. At the center is a billiards table on which one red ball and two white balls sit idle beside a single cue laid across its length. Behind the table stands a man in white, the proprietor of the cafe (I read). He's posing, as if for a photo. The white he wears is not really white, it's more of a luminous yellow-green.

All the tabletops and a bar in the background, a door in a backroom seen through a doorway, even a reflection in a mirror are all painted using variations on this color. These contrast starkly with the blood-red walls. Light from four large gas chandeliers struggles against the oppressive darkness of the room. Van Gogh visualizes this struggle in radiating yellow waves that quiver on the verge of extinction. Bottles and glasses litter the tabletops. Five seated patrons, three of whom appear to be sleeping and two in the back, a man and a woman, who may be engaged in a tryst, are the only other people in the frame. A gigantic brown clock reads 12:10.

I returned to this painting on several occasions, paying attention each time to a different aspect. In my notebook I wrote about the colors, the texture, the composition, the biographical backstory, and anything else I could think of, all with the intention of turning my notes into a poem. The poem never materialized.

On the way to see the Van Gogh one afternoon, I passed a Paul Klee painting called *Joyful Mountain Landscape*. The next morning I wrote a poem in one sitting called *Joyful Mountain Landscape*. Why did this painting lend itself so easily and instantaneously to the writing of a poem while the Van Gogh, which I had looked at and studied so intently, resisted my efforts to translate it into poetry? How is it that I have now composed an entire book of ekphrastic poetry, most of it based on tiny digital reproductions, yet this one painting, which I examined again and again in the flesh, eludes me?

***

(Ars Memoria)

A recording of Louise Bourgeois singing *C'est la murmure d l'eau qui chante* and other French children's rhymes. A vacuum cleaner whirring outside my office door. I recall one of her *Couple*s sculptures at the Albright-Knox Art Gallery in Buffalo. If I mark that spot in my mind, it is easy for me to mentally map the whole museum. I can wander in one direction down a long hall hung with impressionist and post-impressionist paintings (including a work by Seurat) or I can go in another direction through rooms full of pop and op and abstract expressionist art. As I do this I realize that the museum is a kind of memory palace. I could place things on the walls and use them to recall a speech I'd like to give or a list of randomly ordered playing cards. Or I could just wander my own museum, which is built inside of yours.

Notes

Landscape with Figures

Massimo Vitale, *Rosignano 2004 diptych, #1941*

Another White Horse

George Bellows, *The White Horse*, 1922

Portrait of the Poet Iwar Von Lücken
by Otto Dix, 1926

This image appeared in my Facebook feed, posted there
by Russian writer Mikhail Iossel.

Zero Gravity (A Hoax)

Marc Chagall, *Birthday*, 1915

Heliotrope

This poem originated as a collaboration with French
painter and sculptor Isabelle Pellissier. She sent me more
than a hundred of the note cards on which she transcribes
her thoughts while working in her studio. These are
mostly fragmentary and written in French, of which I
speak very little. I ran them through Google Translate and
used the results for inspiration every day for over a year,
hoping to create a text in which her cards came into
conversation with the poems I was writing. Eventually this

other poem took on a life of its own, one that bears little resemblance to the original cards. That said, many of the images and lines are direct translations, false translations, interpretations and elaborations of Isabelle's words and images. I am grateful to her for providing the foundation to these poems.

Michael Kelleher is the author of the poetry collections *Human Scale* and *To Be Sung*, both from BlazeVOX as well as *Visible Instruments*, forthcoming from Chax. From 2008-2013 he produced *Aimless Reading*, a blog project in which he photographed, catalogued, and wrote about the more than 1200 titles in his library. He is the Director of the Windham-Campbell Literature Prizes at Yale University and the former Artistic and Associate Director of Just Buffalo Literary Center in Buffalo, NY.

Made in the USA
Monee, IL
07 July 2026

56552439R00062